LAINEY WILSON:

The Girl with a Big Voice

Kelly J. Fiedler

All rights reserved. No part of this publication may be reproduced, distributed, or transmitted in any form or by any means, including photocopying, recording, or other electronic or mechanical methods, without the prior written permission of the publisher, except in the case of brief quotations embodied in critical reviews and certain other noncommercial uses permitted by copyright law.

Copyright ©Kelly J. Fiedler , 2024:

TABLE OF CONTENTS

INTRODUCTION

CHAPTER 1: WHO IS LAINEY WILSON

CHAPTER 2: GROWING UP IN LOUISIANA

CHAPTER 3: DISCOVERING HER LOVE FOR MUSIC

CHAPTER 4: LEARNING TO PLAY THE GUITAR

CHAPTER 5: SINGING AT LOCAL EVENTS

CHAPTER 6: WRITING HER SONGS

CHAPTER 7: CHASING HER DREAMS IN NASHVILLE

CHAPTER 8: LAINEY'S FIRST BIG HIT

CHAPTER 9: BECOMING A COUNTRY STAR

CHAPTER 10: LAINEY'S AMAZING JOURNEY SO FAR

CONCLUSION

QUIZ TIME

INTRODUCTION

Lainey Wilson grew up in Louisiana's small town of Baskin. Being in the country, with lots of open fields all around her, she quickly learned to love the simple things in life. Lainey liked music ever since she was a little girl. Folk music was important to her family, so she grew up listening to Dolly Parton and Johnny Cash. She hoped one day to be able to sing like them.

The little girl Lainey had learned to play the guitar before she turned nine. Her dad taught her how to play the piano for the first time, and she fell in love with making music right away. She worked out every day and was always trying to learn new songs to play and sing. She loved music so much that it turned into a passion and a way for her to express herself.

Lainey didn't just want to learn how to play music, though. She also wanted to write her songs. When she was a teenager, she began writing down her feelings and thoughts and adding music to them. Her songs were like stories to her, and it was clear that she was very good at making people feel something through them.

Lainey learned that she needed to be in Nashville, Tennessee, where country music was made if she wanted to follow her dreams. Lainey was brave enough to leave her small town and the people she loved and move to Nashville when she was done with school. It wasn't easy, but Lainey knew she had to risk it all to get ahead.

Lainey's life in Nashville wasn't always easy. She had a hard time at first getting her music heard. While she kept writing songs, she put on small shows with very small crowds. Lainey never gave up, though, even though things were hard. She worked hard because she thought her big break was coming one day.

When her first hit song, "Things a Man Oughta Know," came out, she finally got that break. A lot of people felt something from the song, and soon Lainey's name was being talked about all over the country. She had honest lyrics and a strong voice that made her music stand out. People fell in love with it.

Lainey stayed true to herself and her roots as her fame grew. She kept writing music that was personal and important to her. People loved her for it, and her songs went straight to the top of the charts. There was more to Lainey's music than just catchy tunes. She told stories that people could relate to.

Some people say that Lainey is one of the hottest new country music stars. She has won awards, played on big stages, and made fans all over the world. There is no way for Lainey to forget where she came from, though. She will always be connected to her Louisiana roots.

This book tells the story of Lainey Wilson's life, from her childhood in Louisiana to her rise to fame as a country music singer. You'll learn how

Lainey's love of music, hard work, and determination helped her reach her goals.

Are you ready to find out more about the girl who has a big voice? Let's look into Lainey Wilson's amazing life and see how she became one of the most inspiring stars in country music!

CHAPTER 1: WHO IS LAINEY WILSON

Lainey Wilson is a powerful country music singer and songwriter who was born on May 19, 1992. Her powerful voice and honest lyrics have won over many hearts. Lainey was raised in the small Louisiana town of Baskin, where country music was a big part of life from a very young age. This style of music was very important to her family, and she grew up listening to artists like Dolly Parton and Johnny Cash.

Lainey has always been interested in music. With her dad's help, she learned to play the guitar and fell in love with it right away. She became very good at singing and writing songs as she practiced. She often wrote her songs and performed them at local events. Even when she was a teenager, Lainey's skill and hard work were clear.

Realizing that she needed to move to the center of the country music industry to become a star, Lainey chose to move to Nashville, Tennessee. Making the move was a big step, and life in Nashville was hard. Lainey tried to get noticed by playing at small venues, working different jobs, and writing new songs all the time.

Lainey's hard work paid off when she released "Things a Man Oughta Know," her big hit song. A lot of people liked the song, which showed off her unique mix of old-fashioned country and newer sounds. With this hit single, she became known as a new voice in country music and began her rise to fame.

Lainey Wilson quickly became a fan favorite in the country music world thanks to her engaging performances and honest songwriting. People love her music because the lyrics are honest and reflect her values and experiences. One big reason for Lainey's rising popularity is that her songs make people feel like they know her.

Lainey has been praised for both her musical success and her contributions to country music. She has won a lot of awards and praise, which shows how talented and hardworking she is. Lainey is grounded and stays true to her roots, even though she has done a lot.

Lainey's rise from a girl from a small town to a rising star in Nashville shows how hard she works and how much she loves music. Her story shows how to deal with problems and follow your dreams, and many young artists look up to her as an example."

Lainey Wilson's effect on the country music scene grows as she keeps making music and makes big steps forward. Fans are excited to see what comes next for this talented and hardworking artist because her story is far from over.

Aside from being a country music star, Lainey Wilson shows that dreams, hard work, and determination can pay off. From Baskin-Robbins to Nashville, her story shows how to follow your dreams and make a name for yourself in the music world.

CHAPTER 2: GROWING UP IN LOUISIANA

Young Lainey Wilson grew up in Louisiana, where the sounds and culture of the South were always present. There was a lot of community in her small town of Baskin; everyone knew each other. The friendly, warm atmosphere had a big impact on her childhood. Her formative years were set against the beautiful natural scenery of Louisiana, with its lush landscapes and picturesque views.

In Louisiana, Lainey's family was very important to her. They were there for her and encouraged her to do the things she loved, especially music. When Lainey's parents got together with their friends and family, they would play their favorite country songs, so there was always music playing. This early exposure to the genre made her like it and made her want to become a musician.

The arts were alive and well in Baskin, even though it was a small town. There were lots of fairs, festivals, and community events in the area, and live music was often playing. Lainey was excited to go to these events and absorb the performances while learning from the musicians who played. Because of these experiences, she became more interested in music and got a taste of what a music career might be like.

Lainey was raised with a strong sense of family values and education. Her parents told her how important it was to work hard, be dedicated, and follow her dreams. These values were taught to

Lainey from a very young age, and they helped her build a strong future. In every step of her musical journey, from taking lessons to playing at local events, her parents were there for her.

Lainey went to local schools and was an active student when she was young. She took part in school activities and events, which built her confidence and taught her how to speak in public. She got to perform and show off her skills early on by taking part in school plays and musicals, which set the stage for her future music career.

When I was growing up in Louisiana, I was also exposed to a lot of different kinds of music. Lainey heard a lot of different kinds of music, from traditional country to blues and jazz. This wide range of music helped her create her sound and style by combining different styles into her original music.

Lainey also spent a lot of time as a child doing things outside. Louisiana's natural beauty made it easy to have fun outside. Lainey liked going on walks in the country, fishing, and hanging out with her friends. All of these things made her value the little things in life more, and you could hear that in her music.

Lainey's upbringing was shaped by family traditions and events in her community. There was laughter, music, and stories at celebrations and get-togethers. These times not only strengthened family ties but also gave Lainey a sense of belonging and a strong link to her roots.

Lainey grew up in Louisiana, where she felt like she had a strong sense of community and family support. Her upbringing in this lively, musical setting set the stage for her future career. The values she learned, the things she did, and the love of music she found in Louisiana were all important parts of her path to becoming a successful country artist.

Lainey Wilson's upbringing in Louisiana shaped her in lots of ways. A close-knit neighborhood, a loving family, and a lot of music in the area gave her a solid base for her future career. Not only did her time in Louisiana affect her music, but it also gave her the values and drive to follow her dreams and be successful in the country music business.

CHAPTER 3: DISCOVERING HER LOVE FOR MUSIC

Lainey Wilson's love for music began at a very young age. Growing up in the small town of Baskin, Louisiana, Lainey was surrounded by the sounds of country music, which played a significant role in shaping her musical interests. Her family often listened to classic country songs, and these melodies became the soundtrack of her early years. This constant exposure to music sparked a deep passion within her.

From the moment she heard her first country tunes, Lainey was captivated. The stories told through the lyrics and the emotions conveyed through the music resonated with her. She would listen to her favorite songs over and over, learning the words and melodies by heart. This early connection to music laid the foundation for her future career as a singer and songwriter.

Lainey's love for music was further nurtured by her family. They were incredibly supportive of her interests and encouraged her to pursue her passion. Her parents, especially, played a crucial role in her musical development. They took her to local music events and concerts, where she could experience live performances and see musicians in action.

As Lainey grew older, her interest in music only deepened. She started taking music lessons and learning to play instruments. Her fascination with music extended beyond just listening; she wanted to be actively involved in creating it. This desire led her to explore different musical genres and experiment with various instruments.

One of the turning points in Lainey's musical journey was discovering the guitar. The moment she picked up a guitar, she felt a strong connection to it. Strumming the strings and learning chords became a source of joy for her. The guitar became her main instrument, and she spent countless hours practicing and perfecting her skills.

Lainey also began to write her songs, inspired by her love for music. Her songwriting was a way for her to express her thoughts, feelings, and experiences. Each song she wrote was a reflection of her journey and the emotions she wanted to share with others. Her early songs were deeply personal and showcased her natural talent for storytelling.

Her passion for music was not limited to just her own experiences. Lainey actively sought out opportunities to learn from others and expand her musical knowledge. She listened to a wide range of artists, attended workshops, and engaged with the local music community. This eagerness to learn and grow further fueled her love for music.

As Lainey continued to develop her musical skills, she began performing at local events and gatherings. These performances were not only a way for her to showcase her talent but also an opportunity to connect with her audience. Each performance reinforced her love for music and her desire to share it with others.

Lainey's journey in music was marked by both challenges and triumphs. She faced obstacles along the way, but her love for music kept her motivated. Her perseverance and dedication were driven by her deep-rooted passion for music, which never wavered even in the face of adversity.

Through all the ups and downs, Lainey's love for music remained a constant source of inspiration. It guided her through her musical journey and helped her stay focused on her goals. Her passion for music was evident in every song she wrote and every performance she gave.

In time, Lainey's love for music began to pay off. Her talent and dedication were recognized by others, and she started to gain more opportunities in the music industry. Her journey from a small-town girl with a dream to a successful country music artist was a testament to the power of following one's passion.

Today, Lainey Wilson's love for music continues to drive her career. She remains dedicated to her craft, constantly seeking new ways to connect with her audience and share her music. Her journey from discovering her love for music to becoming a country music star is a reminder of the impact that passion and perseverance can have on achieving one's dreams.

CHAPTER 4: LEARNING TO PLAY THE GUITAR

Lainey Wilson's musical journey reached a major turning point when she learned to play the guitar. While she was still young, Lainey was interested in music, and she quickly picked up the guitar as her favorite instrument. Her love of music and determination to learn how to play the guitar made it possible for her to become a successful singer and songwriter.

Acoustic guitar lessons were the first thing Lainey did to learn how to play the guitar. She began by learning simple chords and strumming patterns. As she practiced regularly, her skills got better over time. Lainey was determined to get better at what she did and learn new songs, even though she was just starting.

At first, it was hard to learn how to play the guitar. Lainey had to put in a lot of work to get her fingers stronger and better coordinated. After a long practice session, her fingers would hurt sometimes, but that didn't stop her. She instead saw each problem as a chance to learn and improve as a musician.

From there, Lainey started to try out different styles and techniques as she got better at the basics. She liked a lot of different artists and tried to play like them, which helped her create her sound. She found her musical voice and style through this exploration.

Lainey was able to write better songs after she learned to play the guitar. Once she was good at playing, she started writing her songs, and the guitar became her main tool for making melodies. She was able to be creative and come up with her music ideas because she could play and write music at the same time.

Lainey also looked to other guitarists and musicians for ideas. To learn new skills and get a feel for different playing styles, she went to workshops, watched performances, and listened to recordings. This desire to learn from others kept her motivated and helped her get better at what she did.

Lainey started playing in front of people as her guitar skills got better. She felt more confident as a performer and got to show off her skills by playing live. The guitar was an important part of each performance because it let her connect with the crowd and share her music.

Lainey practiced and worked hard, and it paid off in the end. She got better at playing the guitar, and her shows started to stand out. Her skill and emotion in the music she played gave it more depth, which made her songs even more powerful.

Lainey didn't just learn how to play the guitar for fun; she became very good at it and it became her career. It helped her connect with her fans, show off her creativity, and follow her country music dreams. Lainey's progress with the guitar shows how much she loves and works hard at music.

Lainey Wilson's musical journey began with her learning how to play the guitar. She was able to write, perform, and connect with her audience because of it. The hard work Lainey put into learning and getting better at the guitar made her the successful artist she is now, and her love for the instrument still comes through in her music.

CHAPTER 5: SINGING AT LOCAL EVENTS

An important part of Lainey Wilson's early career was singing at local events. Lainey grew up in the small Louisiana town of Baskin. She loved performing in front of people and would do it whenever she could. She was able to show off her skills and gain confidence as a performer at local events.

Lainey has been going to community events, fairs, and festivals since she was a child. Often, these events took place in her hometown or nearby places, where family and friends could get together. Many people who went thought Lainey's performances were the best part. Her moving songs and lively stage presence left a lasting impression.

These events in her area taught Lainey important things about performing live. She learned how to interact with her audience, deal with stage fright, and change her performances to fit different places. Each event helped her get better and connect with the people who were listening.

Lainey felt supported by her community when she sang at events in her area. She always had excited family, friends, and neighbors ready to cheer her on at her shows. Lainey needed this support so badly; it gave her the drive to keep going after her dreams, even though they were hard.

Lainey started getting more requests to perform at different events as her reputation grew in her community. She played at local concerts, school events, and charity fundraisers, each time introducing a new group of people to her unique style and love of music. Because of these changes, she was able to gain fans and perform more often.

Her original songs were also put to the test when she performed at local events. Lainey often played new songs for the first time, seeing how her fans reacted and making changes to her songs based on what they said. This early exposure helped her grow as a singer and songwriter in a big way.

People who came to local events often didn't have a lot of people, but they liked and supported Lainey's music. Lainey was able to stay motivated and focused on her goals with this help. They were special to her, and she used them as stepping stones to bigger stages and bigger chances.

By singing at local events, Lainey also got to know other musicians and people in the community. She worked with local bands and artists a lot, which helped her learn from their mistakes and grow her music industry network. It helped her as she moved up in her career to have these connections.

Lainey never forgot where she came from, even after she moved to Nashville and started performing on bigger stages. She still liked and valued the experiences she gained by singing at events in her community. The early performances she did were very important to her career and helped her grow as an artist.

Lainey Wilson's path to becoming a country music star began with her singing at local events. These performances gave her important experience, confidence, and support from the community. Additionally, they helped her connect deeply with her fans and set the stage for her future success in the music business.

CHAPTER 6: WRITING HER SONGS

One of the most exciting parts of Lainey Wilson's journey was writing her songs. Lainey has loved making music that shows her feelings and experiences since she was a child. Her songs were more than just pretty tunes; they told stories from her heart. Her love of writing songs became an important part of her country music career.

Lainey used to write songs in her bedroom with her guitar by her side all the time. For hours on end, she would sit and play chords and write lyrics that talked about love, life, and her hometown. Her early songs were very personal and from the heart. They were about her experiences and dreams.

After Lainey moved to Nashville, she kept writing songs, but now she could work with other talented songwriters. Nashville is known for having a lot of people who write songs, and Lainey used that to her advantage. She got better at what she did and tried out new ideas by working with other musicians and songwriters.

Lainey was able to learn from different points of view and styles when she worked with other people. She learned how to write songs in new ways that she probably wouldn't have tried on her own. She also met more musicians and people working in the music business through these collaborations, which helped her grow as an artist.

Lainey had full creative control over her music because she wrote all of her songs. She had the freedom to say what she wanted and stay true to her artistic vision. She wanted this freedom because she wanted her songs to show off her unique voice and her own life. Fans liked how her lyrics often told stories that hit home for them.

One of the hardest things for Lainey about writing songs was coming up with ideas. It would be hard for her to come up with new ideas or get past writer's block sometimes. But Lainey knew that she could get ideas from anyone or anything, like a conversation, a book, or a scene from her daily life. She learned to keep an open mind and pay attention to what was going on around her.

Lainey's songwriting skills kept getting better as her career went on. People started to praise her for being able to write songs with meaningful lyrics and catchy melodies. Her songs not only showed off her talent but also hit home with listeners deeply, which helped her become more well-known.

Writing songs was also an important part of Lainey's live shows. She wrote her songs and played them at all of her concerts. Fans loved hearing the stories behind the songs. Lainey got to share her songs with her audience and get to know them on a personal level at each show.

Lainey's success as a country music singer was due in large part to how hard she worked at writing her songs. In a very competitive field, her ability to make music that was real and relatable helped her stand out. The things she did, the things she loved, and her growth as an artist were all shown in her songs.

As of now, Lainey Wilson is still writing and performing her songs, and her fans still feel moved by them. Her journey as a songwriter shows how powerful creativity can be and how important it is to stay true to yourself. Is Lainey's music just a tune? No, it's the story of her life and her dreams told through her powerful voice.

CHAPTER 7: CHASING HER DREAMS IN NASHVILLE

This is where Lainey Wilson knew she should be when she decided to follow her dreams. Many would-be musicians went to the city, which was known as the "heart of country music," to make their mark. Lainey wasn't any different. She left her small Louisiana town of Baskin, packed her bags, and set out for Music City with hope and determination.

Lainey felt both excited and nervous when she got to Nashville. They were all trying to make it big, and the city was full of them. Lainey knew she had to stand out because the other girls were very good. She started by playing her music in small bars and clubs where anyone could hear it.

Every show was a chance for her to show off her skills and get noticed.

In the beginning, things were hard in Nashville. Lainey often played for small groups, sometimes just a few people. She didn't let that stop her, though. She instead used every chance to get better and connect with the people who were listening. Every time she played, her love for music came through, even when the venue wasn't very full.

Meeting new people was another important part of Lainey's journey. She met other musicians, songwriters, and people who work in the business who could help her get ahead. Lainey was able to get more opportunities by going to music events and making connections with people in the business. These connections were very important for her getting work in Nashville and making a name for herself.

Lainey never lost sight of her goal, even though the competition was tough and there were many problems. She kept writing music and performing, always trying to make her art and music better. She worked hard and dedicated herself, and it paid off when she got more fans and praise for her unique sound and touching songs.

Lainey started to play at bigger venues and festivals as her music became more popular. It was like a dream come true to play for bigger crowds and see her name on event posters. Every show she did was a chance to move her career forward and show more people what she could do.

The music business also noticed how hard Lainey worked. She got offers from record companies and started to record her songs. This was an important moment in her career because it meant that even more people would hear her music. It was exciting for her to start recording her songs because it brought her closer to her goal of becoming a country music star.

Lainey kept her feet on the ground and was thankful for the help she got along the way. She knew that her success wasn't just due to her skills; it was also because her family, friends, and fans cheered her on and helped her. She made it a point to stay close to her roots and thank the people who helped her along the way.

In Nashville, Lainey's journey to follow her dreams was hard but worth it. Her determination and hard work helped her get past problems and reach her objectives. She got closer to her dream of becoming a country music star with each step she took. Her story continues to encourage other people to follow their dreams.

Today, Lainey Wilson's story in Nashville shows how hard work and determination can pay off. She has shown that dreams can come true if you work hard, have passion, and believe in yourself. The success Lainey has had in country music is just the start of a long and exciting career.

CHAPTER 8: LAINEY'S FIRST BIG HIT

Lainey Wilson finally had her big break when she had her first big hit. She had worked hard for years to get there. No matter where you live, that song touched you, and it changed her life forever. This song wasn't like other songs; it was unique. It showed the world how talented Lainey was and told a story that touched people's hearts.

The country sound Lainey is known for was used to make the song about life, love, and staying true to yourself. The song became very popular very quickly because it spoke to a lot of people. More and more people simply couldn't get enough of Lainey's voice and the touching words she had written. It wasn't long before people all over the country could hear the song on the radio.

Lainey's dream came true when she heard her song on the radio for the first time. She had worked hard to get to this point, where her music was being heard by loads of people. For her, it was both an exciting and sad time. She was excited to see where this song would take her next because she knew it would be a big deal in her career.

Lainey's fan base grew as the song went up the charts. Fans began to come from all over the country to hear her music and see her perform. They liked how she stuck to her roots and wrote honest songs with a strong voice. Their favorite thing about Lainey wasn't that she was a singer;

it was that her music told stories, which made her unique.

Lainey's first big hit also helped her get into country music. As she played in bigger places, more people in the music business began to notice how talented she was. She was asked to perform at big country music events, where she shared the stage with some of the finest artists in the business. It meant a lot to her and showed that all her hard work was paying off.

But Lainey stayed humble, even though she had it all. She never forgot where she came from, and the songs she wrote were always based on real events in her life. It wasn't just a one-time hit for her; it was the start of something even bigger. Lainey knew that she would make more great songs if she worked hard.

Lainey saw how much her music meant to people as the song stayed at the top of the charts. People would tell her that the song had helped them get through hard times or reminded them of good times. Lainey was even happier with her music after hearing these stories. It hit her that her songs had the power to change people's lives.

Lainey started getting awards and attention after her first big hit. She was up for a lot of music awards and won some of them. These awards showed how far she had come since her first days in Nashville. Lainey was proud to win these awards, and they also pushed her to keep working hard and making more music.

There was more to Lainey's first big hit than just a song. It was a stepping stone to a better future. The experience gave her the strength to keep going after her goals. She knew this was the start of a very exciting journey in the world of country music.

Lainey is proud of her first big hit. Her big break came with that song, which showed everyone what she could do. But most of all, it made her think about how important it is to work hard, be dedicated, and believe in yourself. That's how Lainey thinks she can keep making great music for years to come.

CHAPTER 9: BECOMING A COUNTRY STAR

She didn't become a country star overnight; Lainey Wilson worked hard, was determined, and loved what she did for years. Lainey has always wanted to be a big star in country music. She knew the journey would be hard, but her love of music and stories helped her stay focused on her goal.

There, Lainey had to show what she could do. She sang her heart out in small venues, to crowds that were sometimes small but always grateful. She learned how to be a better performer and met other musicians and fans who liked her work through these early shows.

Lainey didn't give up when things got tough. She was set on making a name for herself in the country music world.

People began to notice Lainey as she kept writing and performing. She was different from other singers because her style was a mix of old-fashioned country music and modern flair. She wasn't just going with the flow; she was making her way, staying true to the roots of country music while adding her unique sound. Fans loved how honest her lyrics were. They often talked about her family, her life, and growing up in Louisiana.

A song she put out quickly became a big hit, which was her big break. There was something deeply moving about it that made it stand out from other country songs. Lainey's music quickly became popular and could be heard on radio stations all over the country. Fans connected with the touching lyrics and catchy tune. This hit was the start of her rise to fame.

Lainey started playing at bigger venues and festivals as her music became more popular. It was an honor for her to share the stage with some of the biggest names in country music. Her goal was to show everyone what she could do at every performance, and she never missed a chance. Lainey put everything she had into every song, and her fans loved it.

It took more than just performing to become a country star. It took getting to know your fans as well. Lainey always kept her feet on the ground and was thankful for the people who had believed in her from the beginning. She went out of her way to meet her fans, hear their stories, and say thanks for supporting her. By connecting with her fans in this way, she was able to gain loyal fans that are still growing.

Lainey started getting noticed by people in the music business as her career grew. With awards for her songs and performances, she proved that all her hard work had been worth it. Her early days as an actress in a small Louisiana town were marked by each award and nomination that showed how far she had come.

Being a country star wasn't just about fame or awards for Lainey, though. Everyone was welcome to hear her music. made her happy that her songs could make people feel something, like sadness, hope, or happiness. Her goal with her music was always to tell stories, and she stayed true to that even as she grew.

Lainey Wilson is known as one of the biggest names in country music. It wasn't always easy for her to get to the top, but it was worth it. She knows that to be a country star, you need to do more than just have a big hit. You need to be true to yourself, work hard, and never give up on your dreams. When you think about these things, Lainey's future in country music looks better than ever.

CHAPTER 10: LAINEY'S AMAZING JOURNEY SO FAR

It's truly amazing to see how Lainey Wilson became a country music star. It all began in her small Louisiana town of Baskin, where she grew up listening to country music all the time. Lainey knew she wanted to be a singer from a very young age. She would listen to country legends for hours on end and dream of one day telling her own stories through song.

Lainey's love of music grew quickly when she was a child. She learned to play the guitar on her own and started making up her songs. She loved music so much that it was more than just a hobby for her. Lainey would sing at community events because she was always looking for ways to show off her skills. Her family and friends were always there for her and told her to follow her dreams.

Lainey moved to Nashville, the center of country music when she was ready to take the next big step. Leaving the comforts of her hometown for the bright lights of Music City was a huge step for her. Lainey knew she had to be in Nashville if she wanted to make it in the country music business, though.

It wasn't easy to get ahead. Lainey had to work hard to get noticed in Nashville, where she had to start from the bottom and play in small venues. Even when things got hard, she kept playing her guitar and singing her songs. Lainey had faith in herself and her music, which helped her get through the tough times.

Lainey's big break finally came after years of hard work. When she put out her first big hit, it became a fan favorite right away. A lot of people became interested in Lainey's music when her unique voice and honest lyrics got around the world. For the girl from a small town with big hopes, it came true.

Lainey kept getting better as an artist as her music career took off. She played at bigger events, got more fans, and her songs even won awards. Lainey stayed humble, though. She rarely forgot where she came from and always found time to thank her fans for their support and tell them about her journey.

Lainey's amazing journey shows how important it is to work hard, be determined, and stay true to yourself. She didn't skip steps or give up when things got tough. She instead worked hard to get better at what she did, and her hard work paid off. Lainey is now one of the rising stars in country music, and her story continues to inspire others.

Lainey is still getting new music written, performing, and writing songs. She knows that the journey doesn't end with one big hit; it's an adventure that lasts a lifetime. With her talent, heart, and drive, Lainey's amazing journey will go on for years to come, with even more amazing moments along the way.

People who have dreams should remember Lainey's story: never give up. Anything is possible if you work hard and follow your dreams, no matter how hard the road may seem. It's all possible for Lainey Wilson, a girl from Baskin, Louisiana.

CONCLUSION

The story of Lainey Wilson is one of sticking to her goals, following her heart and being true to herself. Lainey's story shows that with hard work and dedication, dreams can come true. She went from being poor in a small Louisiana town to becoming one of the rising stars of country music. Even when things were hard, she never gave up. She always believed in her voice and the stories she had to tell.

Lainey has stayed grounded, true to her roots, and thankful for the support of her family, friends, and fans throughout her career. What does "her big voice" mean? It means both how well she sings and how well she can tell stories that people can relate to. It doesn't matter if Lainey is writing about love, life, or her hometown; her music moves people and gives them hope.

The road to fame for Lainey is far from over. Her future in country music looks brighter than ever as long as she writes songs, performs, and talks to her fans. With skill, hard work, and a love for what you do, she has shown that anything is possible.

Lainey Wilson's story shows that people who have dreams should never give up. Her example shows that being true to yourself and working hard can get you very far. The girl with the big voice, Lainey Wilson, shows that dreams do come true.

QUIZ TIME

1. Where was Lainey Wilson born?

   A) Texas

   B) Louisiana

   C) Georgia

   D) Alabama

2. What instrument did Lainey Wilson learn to play as a child?

   A) Piano

   B) Drums

   C) Guitar

   D) Violin

3. Which small town in Louisiana did Lainey Wilson grow up in?

A) Baton Rouge

B) New Orleans

C) Baskin

D) Shreveport

4. What genre of music is Lainey Wilson most known for?

A) Pop

B) Jazz

C) Country

D) Rock

5. At what type of events did Lainey Wilson first start performing?

A) School plays

B) Local fairs and festivals

C) Concert halls

D) Music studios

6. Which city did Lainey Wilson move to to pursue her music career?

A) Austin

B) Nashville

C) Los Angeles

D) New York City

7. What was one of the challenges Lainey faced while learning to play the guitar?

A) Learning to read music

B) Building finger strength

C) Memorizing lyrics

D) Performing in public

8. What did Lainey Wilson do to overcome writer's block when writing songs?

A) Took a break from music

B) Watched movies

C) Found inspiration from everyday life

D) Asked friends for help

9. What was Lainey Wilson's reaction to her first big hit?

A) She was surprised and excited

B) She was disappointed

C) She ignored it

D) She was nervous and unsure

10. What is one of Lainey Wilson's values that she learned from her family?

A) Always being on time

B) The importance of hard work

C) Playing multiple instruments

D) Staying indoors during bad weather

ANSWERS

1. B) Louisiana
2. C) Guitar
3. C) Baskin
4. C) Country
5. B) Local fairs and festivals
6. B) Nashville
7. B) Building finger strength
8. C) Found inspiration from everyday life
9. A) She was surprised and excited
10. B) The importance of hard work

Made in the USA
Monee, IL
02 April 2025